HOW TO
LIVE
VICTORIOUSLY

"Basic Steps To A Better Life!"

MATTIE NOTTAGE

HOW TO
LIVE
VICTORIOUSLY

"Basic Steps To A Better Life!"

MATTIE NOTTAGE

TABLE OF CONTENTS

———◄◆►———

WHAT IS SALVATION?

We are all born sinners. According to **John 3:7,** in order to go to heaven we must be born again. If we confess our sin God is faithful and just to cleanse us from all unrighteousness.

How do you do this? **Romans 10:9, 10** says if thou wilt confess with thy mouth the Lord Jesus Christ and believe in your heart that God raised Jesus from the dead, thou shalt be saved.

CHAPTER ONE

---◀◆▶---

ABC'S OF SALVATION
Why Do I Need Salvation?

Have you ever been to a place in your life where nothing seemed to be going right? During these difficult times, you may have felt lost, hopeless and somewhat confused. You may have even felt like giving up on everyone and everything. You may have thought that, if there truly was a God, why did He seem distant and unresponsive. You may have even wondered if the God you heard your grandmother talk about, prayed to and went to church to worship, really existed. And, if He did exist, where was He? Did He really care? How can you get His attention?

> ^{15} *The eyes of the Lord are upon the righteous,*
>
> *and his ears are open unto their cry.*
> *(Psalm 34:15)*

In **Psalm 34:15**, the Psalmist David shares a real life-changing kingdom secret revealing that God hears and answers those who have accepted Him and are in right standing with Him. The first step to getting God's attention is accepting Him as Lord and personal Savior. Once you accept Him as your Savior and Ruler, you are saved.

You are now a Christian, submitted to God and on your way to heaven. However, while you are waiting to go to heaven, your salvation also qualifies you for all of the benefits which come along with being led by Him while you are here on earth, just as a parent would lead his child. Once you accept this eternal covenant, you are saying He is now in control of your life and it is His will, as your Heavenly Father, that you will seek to fulfill.

UNDERSTANDING THE GIFT OF SALVATION?

The Greek word for salvation is *sozo*, which means to be saved from; to rescue from danger or destruction; to deliver from penalty or save from evil; to make well. In the Christian definition, salvation means to be saved from the consequences of sin. The evilness of sin causes you to be separated from a holy God. This separation ultimately leads to spiritual death.

Sin causes you to disobey the laws of God and to go against His commandments. This disobedience and rebelling bring the judgement of God upon your life. Because God is holy, man's sin in the Garden of Eden separated humanity from Him. Although He had to judge the sin, God still loved the Man and wanted to restore His relationship with mankind.

THE PLAN OF SALVATION

⁴ But when the fulness of the time was come, God sent forth His Son, made of a woman, made under the law,

⁵ To redeem them that were under the law, that we might receive the adoption of sons. (Galatians 4:4 – 5)

The Bible says in *Hebrews* **9:22** that without the shedding of blood there is no remission or forgiveness of sin. Remember, sin brings the judgement of death upon the life of the offender. Since the life of every living thing is in the blood, the shedding of blood of a sacrificial animal, symbolically meant the life of that animal would be taken instead of the life of the one who is guilty of the sin.

In order to bring about salvation throughout the ages and through all eternity, it was necessary that a perfect sacrifice be made; one that Heaven and earth would respect and acknowledge from generation to generation.

The Word of God says that in the fullness of time, God sent His Son, His only Son, Jesus to shed His blood and die on the cross so man's soul could be redeemed and bought back from the judgment of eternal death.

When we make the bold confession to accept the blood sacrifice that Jesus made when He died on the Cross, and declare His Lordship over our lives; our sins are forgiven, we are reconciled back to God and we are saved from the eternal consequences of sin, which is death **(Romans 6:23).**

THE WAY TO SALVATION

Whenever you hear and are convicted by the message of the gospel of the Cross and how Jesus gave His life for you, the process of salvation has begun. As you continue to understand that you have missed the mark of holiness and His standard for your life, the feelings of wrongdoings generally lead you to repentance. This conviction and repentance take place because the Holy Spirit of God is now upon you. Conviction means to feel sorry in your heart for what you have done wrong and godly sorrow leads you to repentance.

Repentance is the act of seeking God's forgiveness by changing your mindset, your way of believing, your way of living, and asking Jesus Christ to show you the way of pleasing the Father. Your salvation is then sealed in the blood of Jesus Christ as you denounce the rulership of Satan. This daily commitment to live according to the precepts of God causes you to develop a holy and godly lifestyle.

The life that you are now living by faith in what God says you should do, how God says you should live and His plan for your life causes you to come into right standing with God.

You position yourself for His unmerited favor and blessing which causes you to lead an abundant life.

The ABC's of Salvation (Romans 10:9, 10):

- **A**cknowledge that you are a sinner.

- **B**elieve that Jesus shed His blood and died for you.

- **C**onfess that God has raised Jesus from the grave and He is Lord of your life.

PRAYER FOR SALVATION

If you are not saved, open your mouth and pray the following prayer aloud:

Father God, have mercy upon me this day according to your loving kindness and your tender mercies; blot out my transgressions and my iniquities **(Psalm 51:1).** *Lord Jesus, I repent of every sin in my life. Please forgive me, wash me with your blood from the inside out, and cleanse me from ALL unrighteousness* **(1 John 1:9).** *Jesus I confess with my mouth and believe in my heart that You died and rose from the dead that I might be saved* **(Romans 10:9).** *Jesus, I accept and declare that you are Lord and Savior over my life.*

I denounce Satan as lord over my life and take back ALL of the power over my life that I had given to him, in Jesus' name.

Lord Jesus come into my heart today and baptize me with your Holy Spirit and fire so that I may come into the knowledge of who You are. Form yourself in me, Lord Jesus. I thank You that You are saving me, even as I cry out to You for Your Word says that they who call upon the name of the Lord shall be saved **(Acts 2:21)**. *Father, I thank you that it is by Your grace that I am saved this day* **(Acts 15:11),** *in Jesus' precious and Holy name I pray, AMEN!*

MY SPIRITUAL BIRTHDAY

---◄◆►---

NOW THAT YOU HAVE PRAYED THIS PRAYER, YOU ARE A CHILD OF GOD, A BORN AGAIN BELIEVER...A CHRISTIAN!

I, _____
        (print name)

gave my life to the Lord

on _____/_____/_____
        (insert date here)

located at

_____

_____

(Insert Address, City, State & Zip)

_____

PRAYER FOR REDEDICATION

If you are backslidden or if you have turned back on God, prayer this prayer out loud to come back in right relationship with Him:

Father God, have mercy upon me this day according to your loving kindness and your tender mercies; blot out my transgressions and my iniquities **(Psalm 51:1).** *Lord Jesus, I repent for turning my back on you. Please forgive me. Wash me with your blood and cleanse me from ALL unrighteousness.*

I want to come back to You, O Lord. You said in your Word that You are married to the backslider. Just as the Prodigal son returned to his father, so am I running back to you. Thank You for Your mercy and Your grace. Thank you for loving me Lord. I rededicate my whole life back to You, in Jesus Mighty Name…Amen!

MY SPIRITUAL REDEDICATION DAY

◄◆►

NOW THAT YOU HAVE PRAYED THIS PRAYER, YOUR LIFE HAS BEEN REDEDICATED BACK TO GOD.

I, _____
(print name)

gave my life back to the Lord

on _____/_____/_____
(insert date here)

located at

_____

_____
(Insert Address, City, State & Zip)

_____

PRAYER FOR THE BAPTISM OF THE HOLY GHOST & FIRE

If you are a believer and wish to be baptized in the Holy Ghost and Fire, pray this prayer:

Father God, I am grateful that you saved me and delivered me from all of my sins. I want to grow in the things of God and to be led by the Spirit of God.

I pray that you would baptize my in the Holy Ghost with Fire. I pray to be filled with Your Holy Spirit with the evidence of speaking in tongues, in the mighty name of Jesus. Overtake me Holy Ghost! Overshadow me Holy Spirit and take control of my life. I receive the baptism of the Holy Spirit, now in Jesus mighty name...Amen!

THE BAPTISM OF THE HOLY GHOST & FIRE

◄╫►

NOW THAT YOU HAVE PRAYED THIS PRAYER, YOU ARE NOW FILLED WITH THE HOLY GHOST & FIRE!

I, _____
(print name)

received the Baptism of
the Holy Ghost

on _____/_____/_____
(insert date here)

located at

_____

_____
(Insert Address, City, State & Zip)

_____

CHAPTER TWO

◄◆►

WELCOME TO YOUR NEW LIFE IN CHRIST

You have just made the best decision of your life. Becoming a true child of God means you must now learn a new way of living. You must be willing to turn away from all of your sins.

¹ Wherefore seeing we also are compassed about with so great a cloud of witnesses, let us lay aside every weight, and the sin which doth so easily beset us, and let us run with patience the race that is set before us,

² Looking unto Jesus the author and finisher of our faith; who for the joy that was set before him endured the cross, despising the shame, and is set down at the right hand of the throne of God. (Hebrews 12: 1-2)

That means you must lay aside all of your bad habits and seek God to develop new Christ-like habits. For example: As a born again Christian, your body now belongs to the Holy Spirit, so anything that can bring harm or cause you to stumble in your Christian faith should be avoided.

Some bad habits include, but are not limited to:

- Sexual immorality or lewd behavior, various kinds of acts of promiscuity; homosexuality, lesbianism, bestiality, etc.

- The use of profanity and other vulgar language or behavior

- Riotous living or a partying lifestyle

- Smoking any and all forms of drugs, including marijuana, cocaine, methamphetamines; the excessive use or abuse of prescription drugs, alcoholic beverages and anything that may cause intoxication.

Please also note that the continued practice of such behaviors can open doors in your life to demonic possession.

Jesus wants you to turn away from these and all other bad or destructive habits and behaviors which hinder you from living your best life ever.

THE BASICS OF SALVATION

During your early stages of salvation, there are some terms relative to your Christian faith with which you should become familiar. The following terms are simply explained so that you can receive a basic understanding of the doctrine of salvation.

❖**Redemption** – To redeem means to win or to buy back. When sin entered mankind, God judged us and separated us from Himself. God did not hate us. He loves us but hates sin. Therefore, in the Bible, it says that in the fullness of time, God sent His only Son Jesus to die so He could redeem us and save us from the penalty that sin brings, which is separation from and the judgment of God.

The shedding of Jesus' blood was a sacrifice worthy of God to forgive mankind of sin. The plan of redemption was an agreement that once the blood of Jesus was offered up as a sacrifice, no other sacrifice was necessary. Jesus' life for ours. No more blood needed to be shed. Once an individual accepts Jesus' sacrifice, he is now redeemed and there is nothing else that man needs to do to have his sins forgiven and be reconciled back to God **(Genesis 3:17; 1 Corinthians 1:30; Romans 8:2)**

THE REDEMPTIVE WORK OF CHRIST ON THE CROSS

To *redeem* means to buy back or win back something that you once had, but was lost. Jesus' death, burial and resurrection were all a part of God's strategic plan to undo the sin Adam and Eve had committed, causing them to lose their spiritual position with God in the Garden of Eden. In the Garden, Adam was a spiritual being with the highest level of delegated authority to operate.

Whatever name Adam gave the animals, is what their names became. He was given this authority by God and did so in the spirit of God.

Adam communed with God daily. He spent so much time with

Him that he knew His spirit and was able to function like Him until he was deceived by the trick of the serpent and, with his wife, Eve, disobeyed God. This disobedience caused them to lose their relationship with God and brought the judgement of God upon them.

Both Adam and Eve were exiled out of the garden which represented the presence of God and lost their spiritual authority in the earth. God immediately devised a plan to restore Man back to his rightful place with Him. This plan of redemption would require the ultimate sacrifice of His Son, Jesus. The ultimate sacrifice that would seal the halls of judgement throughout eternity.

The plan of redemption was established on three basic premises:

1)*Man is sinful.* The sin in Man's nature separates him from a Holy God and ultimately leads to death. This death leads to difficulty and hardship here on earth and ultimately to an eternal life separated from God.

2)*There is nothing that Man in his sinful state can do to please a Holy God.* However, as a new or born again Believer, you can please God in so many ways. Religion, good works, nor any of Man's efforts can make him worthy of a relationship with God. The Word of God reveals that all have sinned and come short of the glory of God. **(Romans 3:23)** God without man is God, but man without God is lost.

3)*Jesus' sacrifice on the Cross reconciles Man back to God.* God loves His Son Jesus. Therefore, all those who accept Jesus receives the acceptance of the Father. A Cross was used as the place of sacrifice because it represented the bridging of a connection between heaven and earth; the prophecy of the Old Testament or old covenant and Jesus being the manifested fulfillment and negotiator of a new covenant. The Word of God says that the first Adam was a living soul or who was alive but the second Adam, who was Jesus, became a quickening spirit, one who is able to make alive or bring to life. **(1 Corinthian 15:45)**

THE PATHWAY TO REDEMPTION

The pathway to redemption involves several foundational truths that you should always remember. Some of these include, but are not limited to the following:

❖**Repentance** - Turning away from sin by changing one's mindset and actions to obey the principles of the Bible. The repentance process consists of feeling sincere regret or sorrow for doing wrong, confessing the sin(s), asking for forgiveness, making amends for any damage done, and putting mechanisms in place so as not to repeat the sin.

❖**Reconciliation** - The ministry of reconciliation is the process of uniting two estranged or divided parties, in this case; a holy God and sinful man. Man has greatly offended and displeased God by his sin of casting off allegiance to Him, rebelling against Him, ignoring His authority, or transgressing against His commandments. This sin has caused a breach between God and man, which has created much hostility instead of friendship; enmity instead of amity; separation and alienation instead of harmony and agreement. Therefore, there is a need for peace to be made between the estranged parties, that the wrong may be righted, the cause of the displeasure be removed, the ill-feelings caused to cease, and the breach between the two be totally healed. Then and only then can true reconciliation be restored in the relationship. **(Ephesians 2:13, Colossians 1:21-22)**

❖**Salvation** – To be saved from the consequences of sin which is separation from God and His divine will for your life. This disunity in your relationship with God, if prolonged, will lead to not only spiritual death, but can also lead to an untimely natural death. **(Ephesians 2:8-9; Hebrews 7:25; Romans 10:9-13; Acts 4:12).**

❖**Deliverance** - To be totally set free from something; to be released; to escape; to rescue or it can also mean to bring into freedom. Deliverance comes from the Greek word *soteria*, whose root word is *sozo* meaning salvation or to save someone or something from danger. Therefore, deliverance represents a higher level of salvation. Sometimes your deliverance can take place immediately **(Luke 18:35-43) or can manifest over a period of time. (Mark 8:22-26)**.

❖**Sanctification** – To be set aside from something (sin, worldly ambitions, ungodly behavior); to be set aside unto something (God's purpose and plan for your life). *Sanctification* has nothing to do with the behaviors, beliefs, actions, or spirituality of the believer, but everything to do with the free grace of a loving and merciful God. *scriptures* **(Galatians 2:20, 1 Thessalonians 4 :3 and 5:23)**

❖**Regeneration** – To generate something means to produce

something or to bring it into being. When you accept Christ, you become born again or born as a new person with new perspectives, new ideas or beliefs; overall, a new way of living. A new born baby has all of its fingers, toes, hands, legs and vital organs. However, it takes time for the baby to mature and for all of its limbs to become strong and fully developed. As a new believer, there are parts of your character, belief system, way of doing things and other behaviors that must be changed. This change takes place from the inside and is demonstrated on the outside.

The process of this type of transformation is known as regeneration. In other words, *regeneration* or being born again, occurs when the grace of God comes to you in your dead state, inability, in the weakness of your flesh, and does for you that which you are incapable of doing. **A Holy God comes to you in your unregenerate state and gives you life.** As you begin to learn more about God and what He expects from you, you will encounter behaviors and attitudes in your spirit that go against what God wants you to display.

As you continue to grow as a Christian, you will begin to

identify more and more of these types of negative attitudes and behaviors. The Word of God reveals in *Romans 8:1*, the Spirit of God does not condemn you for such attitudes or behaviors, as long as your desire is to seek out these attributes which do not please Him and to pray against them so that the Holy Spirit will give you the power to overcome them.

God does not condemn you because they are there, but He does make you accountable once they are revealed to you, but you choose to either deny them or to do nothing about them. These *unregenerated* parts of your spirit man can only become more and more like God by reading His Word and spending time in His presence through prayer **(Titus 3:5; Ephesians 2:1; Romans 6:11).**

❖**Justification** – This is a benefit of being a child of God or a believer.   To justify someone means to validate, defend, and give reason for or to substantiate. When God saved you, He set you aside (sanctification) for His purpose. You are justified through Christ Jesus by God's grace and supernaturally placed into right standing with your Creator and the Creator of mankind. Christians are justified solely based on identifying with the righteousness of our Lord and Savior, Jesus the Christ. This justification is not based on anyone's personal merit. It is in fact, the Spirit of God that brings about justification, whereby God no longer sees you in the light of your imperfections, but He sees you as someone for who Christ died. While you are justified and you have been set aside, there are still "unrejuvenated" areas in your life.

However, He no longer condemns you for your shortcomings and even defends you against the accusations of your enemies as He continues to bring you into a state of perfection. **(Romans 5:1; Galatians 2:16-17; Romans 3:20; Galatians 3:11; Romans 8:29-31).**

CHAPTER THREE

————◀╬▶————

YOU ARE SAVED...NOW WHAT?

"Therefore, if anyone is in Christ, he is a new creation; old things are passed away; behold, all things have become new."
(2 Corinthians 5:17)

Now that you are saved, you must put away everything ungodly that reminds you of your life before becoming a Christian. This includes anything that would not be pleasing to God, such as fornication, deception, profanity, rage, riotous behavior or any other behavior that does not honor a holy God. The Bible teaches that you are to lay aside every weight and the sin that can cause you to stumble as a Christian.

Wherefore seeing we also are compassed about with so great a cloud of witnesses, let us lay aside every weight, and the sin which doth so easily beset us, and let us run with patience the race that is set before us,... **(Hebrews 12:1)**

The race that the Bible speaks of in *Hebrews 12:1,* simply refers to the Christian walk that God has pre-ordained for you to walk in. There is a pathway for you and purpose for you to fulfill. You must now spend your days seeking out this pathway and going after the will of God for your life.

In order to do this, you must also denounce your ties to Satan and declare that he is no longer lord of your life, but that Jesus is now your Lord and Savior. Your life's goal is to please Him. You must realize that you are a new person with new goals, responsibilities, standards and a new outlook on life. You can no longer live, act and function as others in the world do. You must realize that as a Christian you are not your own, you were bought with a price. You now belong to God and you have given Christ full authority over your life **(Ephesians 1:7; Matthew 26:28).** You must also realize that as a Christian your focus is now on heavenly and spiritual matters, not earthly and sensual ones.

HOW TO GROW AS A CHRISTIAN

In order for you to begin to grow in the knowledge of God, it is important you get connected to a

Bible-believing Church that teaches about the work and demonstration of the Holy Spirit. Over the years, we personally have come to understand the importance of the working of the Holy Spirit in the life of each believer if you are going to remain faithful in your walk with God.

12 And we beseech you, brethren, to know them which labour among you, and are over you in the Lord, and admonish you;

13 And to esteem them very highly in love for their work's sake. And be at peace among yourselves.
(1 Thessalonians 5:12-13)

It is also important that you seek out Pastors who have the heart of God and who are willing to teach you the things of God. The Word of God also admonishes that you should "know them that labor among you."

As a result, we have established a Miracles at Midnight daily broadcast where we teach Kingdom principles and truths which help believers all around the world to build their faith in God. These broadcasts are available on all of our Social Media platforms, such as YouTube @ mattienottagetv and on Facebook @ Prophetess Mattie Nottage and Twitter @ DrMattieNottage. We also have lots of resources available through our Official Ministry website at mattienottage.org and through our Ministry App; available through the Android and Apple App stores. We offer these and many other resource tools which will help you grow spiritually.

Stay Connected

In **Hebrews 10:25**, the Word of God admonishes us that we should not forsake the assembling of ourselves together. In unifying and staying connected to other believers, you will find the strength you need to continue on your spiritual walk with God.

As you grow in the things of God, you should continue to ponder on things that are true, honest, just, pure, and of good report and on making going to heaven your primary concern. **(Philippians 4:8; Colossians 3:1-4)**

As a symbol of your conversion experience, every believer is required to participate in water baptism. It is one of the ordinances of the Church and a Christian practice that you need to understand.

UNDERSTANDING THE SIGNIFICANCE OF WATER BAPTISM?

The Ordinance of Baptism by immersion in water is commanded in the Scriptures. All who repent and believe on Jesus Christ as Savior and Lord are to be baptized. Thus, they declare to the world that they have died with Christ and have also been raised with Him to walk in the newness of life. It is a life that God has predestined you to live and walk in.

WHY IS IT IMPORTANT?

The Ordinance of Baptism is important because this act of obedience seals your personal commitment with God. The act of being baptized symbolizes that you are willing to let go of and die to your old way of doing things; your coming up out of the water symbolizes that you have risen as a new person in Jesus Christ; you covenant that you will no longer live according to your old ways, customs and beliefs but you will embrace a new life in God.

AFTER BAPTISM WHAT IS EXPECTED OF YOU?

After you are baptized, God sees you as a brand, new creature. He has a plan for your life that will cause you to be blessed and prosper in every area of your life.

This new life requires that you live your life according to the teachings of the Bible. This dedication to live a life separate from what the world dictates and based on the principles of His Word brings you into holy living.

God is holy. The Word teaches us that we are to be holy as He is holy. Salvation changes the way you live and causes you to desire to live more and more like Him. The more you begin to change and become more like Him, the more you attract the presence of God to your life.

BAPTISM OF THE HOLY SPIRIT

"I indeed baptize you with water unto repentance. but he that cometh after me is mightier than I, whose shoes I am not worthy to bear: he shall baptize you with the Holy Ghost, and with fire: (Matthew 3:11)

There are two basic types of baptisms that you should experience as a born again believer. Water baptism brings you into salvation and the baptism of the Holy Spirit that helps you maintain your salvation. As we saw earlier, water baptism is an ordinance of the Church and is required for every believer who gives their life to the Lord.

During water baptism, you are totally submerged under water and then you come up out of the water as a new person. You are symbolically burying your old sinful nature and are being washed with water into a new life.

Further, as you are submerged, you are no longer seen. Your new commitment is that you will no longer live according to what you want, how you feel or what you think, but you will now be led by the Spirit of God. This is why it is so important for you to read your Bible so that you will begin to learn about how God wants you to live your life.

As you continue your new walk of faith, which is lived no longer by what you see, hear or feel in the natural, you will need to learn how to live spiritually, by having faith in God and in His Word.

The only way for you to truly live victoriously as a Christian is to be baptized with the Holy Ghost and fire. **(Matthew 3:11)** When you are baptized with the Holy Ghost, you are totally taken over by the Spirit of God and it is the Holy Spirit that now lives in and through you.

Holy Spirit will now speak to you concerning the things that you are to do. He will order your steps, show you how to conduct yourself, and even teach you how to speak as a Christian. The Holy Spirit will help you communicate with God, the Father. He is the mediator of your relationship. He helps you to commune with God. He speaks the language of God and He also speaks your language. He intercedes for you. He leads and guides you in paths of truth and righteousness. He reveals to you the will of the Father. He convicts you of actions, attitudes or beliefs which are displeasing to the Father. The presence of the Holy Spirit in your life is your spiritual seal here on earth that sanctions you for eternity.

Yes, to truly live victoriously as a Christian, you need the Holy Ghost. Ask Him to baptize you. Seek out His baptism so that you can please God every day as you walk by faith.

SCRIPTURES ABOUT THE HOLY GHOST

1) HOLY GHOST IS A GIFT TO THE BODY OF CHRIST

ACTS 2:38

Then Peter said unto them, Repent, and be baptized every one of you in the name of Jesus Christ for the remission of sins, and ye shall receive the gift of the Holy Ghost.

2) HOLY GHOST IS AN ETERNAL SEAL OF SALVATION TO THE BELIEVER

EPHESIANS 4:30

Grieve not the holy Spirit of God, whereby ye are sealed unto the day of redemption.

3) HOLY SPIRIT INTERCEDES AND MEDIATES FOR US ACCORDING TO THE WILL OF GOD, THE FATHER

ROMANS 8:26

Likewise, the Spirit also helpeth our infirmities: for we know not what we should pray for as we ought: but the Spirit itself maketh intercession for us with groanings which cannot be uttered

ROMANS 8:27

And he that searcheth the hearts knoweth what is the mind of the Spirit, because he maketh intercession for the saints according to the will of God.

4) HOLY GHOST IS AN EMPOWERMENT OF THE ANOINTING OF GOD

ACTS 1:8

But ye shall receive power, after that the Holy Ghost is come upon you: and ye shall be witnesses unto me both in Jerusalem, and in all Judaea, and in Samaria, and unto the uttermost part of the earth.

5) THE HOLY GHOST IS GOD DWELLING IN US

1 CORINTHIANS 6:19-20

What? know ye not that your body is the temple of the Holy Ghost which is in you, which ye have of God, and ye are not your own? For ye are bought with a price: therefore, glorify God in your body, and in your spirit, which are God's.

6) HOLY GHOST IS A REVEALER OF THE THINGS OF GOD

1 CORINTHIANS 2:11

For what man knoweth the things of a man, save the spirit of man which is in him? even so the things of God knoweth no man, but the Spirit of God.

7) HOLY GHOST IS A COMFORTER AND TEACHER OF THE THINGS OF GOD

JOHN 14:26

But the Comforter, which is the Holy Ghost, whom the Father will send in my name, he shall teach you all things, and bring all things to your remembrance, whatsoever I have said unto you.

8) HOLY GHOST ACTIVATES THE ANOINTING

ACTS 2:3,4

And there appeared unto them cloven tongues like as of fire, and it sat upon each of them. And they were all filled with the Holy Ghost, and began to speak with other tongues, as the Spirit gave them utterance.

9) HOLY GHOST IS AN EMPOWERMENT TO THE BELIEVER TO DO THE WILL OF GOD

MATTHEW 28:19, 20

Go ye therefore, and teach all nations, baptizing them in the name of the Father, and of the Son, and of the Holy Ghost; teaching them to observe all things whatsoever I have commanded you: and, lo, I am with you always, even unto the end of the world. Amen.

10) HOLY GHOST IS AN EMPOWERMENT OF SPIRITUAL GIFTS (THE PROPHETIC, MIRACLES, THE SUPERNATURAL)

ACTS 19:5-6

When they heard this, they were baptized in the name of the Lord Jesus. And when Paul had laid his hands upon them, the Holy Ghost came on them; and they spake with tongues, and prophesied.

CHAPTER FOUR

---◄╫►---

THE BELIEVERS' WORSHIP

"Why We Do What We Do"

As you grow in Christ, you will begin to learn how to walk, think and act like a believer. You will also begin to learn more about the King who you now serve and the Kingdom of which you are a part. You will begin to learn the customs and practices of how to worship and give praise to your God.

Our God is a triune being: God, the Father; God, the Son; and God, the Holy Spirit. God, our Heavenly Father, is reigning upon His throne which is established in the third dimension. Jesus the Son, took on human flesh, came to earth, sacrificed His life and died for us all so that we could have a right to live. When Jesus left, He left the Spirit of God, or God the Holy Spirit, with us who would dwell within us as a spiritual compass and a guide who would lead us into the right ways and paths of the Father. Therefore, we pray to God the Father, in the name of Jesus, the Christ and trust the Holy Spirit to bring to pass what we have requested.

During our worship services, we freely express our honor, love and adoration to our Lord and Savior Jesus Christ who is our King and the One who we now serve. Every act of worship that we practice is written and supported in the Bible, which we call the Word of God or the Scriptures. At times people ask us why we do what we do:

1) **Why do we read from the Bible during our worship services?** (*NOTE:** We recommend that you read the King James Version or the Amplified Version of the Bible.

   SCRIPTURE: 2 Timothy 3:16-17
   All scripture is given by inspiration of God, and is profitable for doctrine, for reproof, for correction, for instruction in [the ways of] righteousness:

2) **Why do we clap our hands during our worship services?**

   SCRIPTURE: Psalm 47:1
   O clap your hands, all ye people; shout unto God with the voice of triumph.

3) **Why do we dance during our worship services?**

SCRIPTURE: 2 Samuel 6:14
And David danced before the Lord with all his might; and David was girded with a linen ephod.

4) **Why we play musical instruments during our praise and worship?**

SCRIPTURE: Psalm 150:4
Praise him with the timbrel and dance: praise him with stringed instruments and organs.

5) **Why do we participate in communion?**

SCRIPTURE: 1 Corinthians 11:24-26

[24] And when he had given thanks, he brake it, and said, Take, eat: this is my body, which is broken

for you: this do in remembrance of me.

25 After the same manner also he took the cup, when he had supped, saying, this cup is the new testament in my blood: this do ye, as oft as ye drink it, in remembrance of me.

26 For as often as ye eat this bread, and drink this cup, ye do shew the Lord's death till he come.

6) Why do we sing and shout clamorous praises to our God?

SCRIPTURE: Psalm 100:1-2
1 Make a joyful noise unto the Lord, all ye lands.

² Serve the Lords with gladness; come before His presence with singing.

SCRIPTURE: Psalm 48:1
Great is the Lord, and greatly to be praised in the city of our God, in the mountain of his holiness.

7) Why do we pray in tongues?

SCRIPTURE: 1 Corinthians 14:2
For he that speaketh in an unknown tongue speaketh not unto men, but unto God: for no man understandeth him; howbeit in the spirit he speaketh mysteries.

8) Why do we give tithe and offering?

SCRIPTURE: Malachi 3:10

Bring ye all the tithes into the storehouse, that there may be meat in mine house, and prove me now herewith, saith the Lord of hosts, if I will not open you the windows of heaven, and pour you out a blessing, that there shall not be room enough to receive it.

CHAPTER FIVE

———◄┃◆┃►———

BUILDING YOUR FAITH AS A BELIEVER

Your new life in Christ begins as soon as you accept Him as Lord and Savior. Once you are saved, it is time to live as a believer or a follower of Christ. Ephesians 2:1-10 will help you understand how to begin to grow in the things of God and understand what God saved you from and what He has saved you to.

The Plan of Salvation as outlined in Ephesians 2:1-10...

YOU ARE MADE ALIVE BY JESUS'S SACRIFICE WHICH SEPARATED YOU FROM SIN

1 And you hath he quickened, who were dead in trespasses and sins;

YOU NO LONGER LIVE ACCORDING TO WORLDY STANDARDS

2 Wherein in time past ye walked according to the course of this world, according to the prince of the power of the air, the spirit that now worketh in the children of disobedience:

YOU ARE NOT THE ONLY SINNER...ALL HAVE SINNED AND COME SHORT OF GOD'S GLORY.

3 Among whom also we all had our conversation in times past in the lusts of our flesh, fulfilling the desires of the flesh and of the mind; and were by nature the children of wrath, even as others.

YOU HAVE RECEIVED SALVATION BECAUSE OF THE MERCIES AND LOVE OF GOD

4 But God, who is rich in mercy, for his great love wherewith he loved us,

YOU ARE SAVED BY GOD'S GRACE…NOT BY ANYTHING YOU HAVE DONE

5 Even when we were dead in sins, hath quickened us together with Christ, (by grace ye are saved;)

YOU CAN BEGIN TO ELEVATE IN THE THINGS OF GOD

6 And hath raised us up together, and made us sit together in heavenly places in Christ Jesus:

YOU CAN EXPERIENCE THE FULLNESS OF THE GOODNESS AND GRACE OF GOD BECAUSE OF JESUS' SACRIFICE

7 That in the ages to come he might shew the exceeding riches of his grace in his kindness toward us through Christ Jesus.

YOU ARE SAVED BY YOUR FAITH IN GOD...THIS IS THE GIFT OF SALVATION

8 For by grace are ye saved through faith; and that not of yourselves: it is the gift of God:

YOU ARE NOT SAVED BASED ON WHAT YOU DO OR HOW YOU FEEL

9 Not of works, lest any man should boast.

YOU ARE NOW EQUIPPED TO LIVE A HOLY LIFE...THIS IS YOUR BEST LIFE EVER

10 For we are his workmanship, created in Christ Jesus unto good works, which God hath before ordained that we should walk in them.

MAINTAINING YOUR SALVATION

Any well trained mechanic would tell you that in order for your vehicle to operate effectively, it needs regular maintenance. Likewise, in your Christian walk, there are some daily check-ups or check points that you must observe in order to live your Christian life to the fullest and become all that God has ordained for you to become. First, the following facts about your salvation must be underscored.

1) YOU ARE SAVED BY FAITH.

Your salvation is based upon your faith in Jesus Christ as your Lord and Savior. In other words, salvation is not something that can be "earned" by how good you try to be or some religious act that you perform. Salvation is a free gift from God, and came as you simply put your faith in Jesus, His death and resurrection and trusted Him to forgive you of your sins and become your Lord and Savior. The scripture says *"For it is by grace you have been saved, through faith; and this is not from yourselves, it is the gift of God; not by works, so that no one can boast"* *(Ephesians 2:8-9).*

2) YOU ARE NOT SAVED BASED ON HOW YOU FEEL. Good feelings are pleasant to have, but feelings do not prove whether you are saved or not. There may be times when you feel that God is close to you and other times when you feel that He is not. Remember He has promised to always be with you and never leave you, regardless of how you feel **(*Hebrews 13:5*).** Always remember that Christians live by faith not by sight or the feelings of our natural senses.

3) YOU ARE NOT PERFECT, JUST FORGIVEN BY THE GRACE OF GOD. Being a Christian does not mean that you would not make mistakes, but it does means that you are forgiven of sin and your goal is to live like Christ and not in the old sinful way anymore. Do not ever let the devil condemn you if you stumble or make a mistake! God loves you and wants you to ask Him to forgive you *(1 John 1:9)*. Jesus wants you to get back on your feet and keep walking for Him. Do not allow others or the Devil to bring condemnation upon you! God loves you and will correct you, but He will not condemn you to make you feel guilty. He will convict you, however, to make you feel the need to repent and change your actions. *"There is now no condemnation for those who are in Christ Jesus..." (Romans 8:1).*

4) **YOU ARE A NEW CREATION.** At the moment you accepted Jesus, He came into your heart by His Spirit and now His presence and nature lives and dwells within your heart *(1 Corinthians 6:19).* You did not merely become a better person, you were "Born again" spiritually as a brand new person! Now, He wants you to learn to live your life according to the new nature of His Spirit inside you. The Word of God also reveals in **2 Corinthians 5:17,** *"Therefore if anyone is in Christ, he is a new creation: the old has gone, the new has come!"* This simply means that you no longer see life the way you saw it before you became a Christian. The more you grow in Christ, the more you will begin to see

life through His eyes. Not only will you begin to see life differently, but you will also begin to walk in blessings reserved for those who made the same decision that you did; to give your life to Him and follow after His purpose and will for your life. You now also have a promise of living an eternal life with Him in Heaven throughout all eternity.

5) READ YOUR BIBLE EVERY DAY. The Bible must be read daily. It is like food for the "new you". It is like milk that a baby drinks. Finally, it is like vitamins to keep you strong and healthy (*Psalms 1:2-3*). A healthy baby has a healthy appetite. If you have truly been "born" of the Spirit of God, you will have a healthy appetite for the things of God. The

Bible says, "As newborn babes, desire the pure milk of the word, that you may grow thereby," *(1 Peter 2:2)*. Feed yourself every day without fail. Job said, ***"I have treasured the words of His mouth more than my necessary food," (Job 23:12)***. The more you eat, the quicker you will grow. The Bible is God's Word, and as you read from it every day, it will cause you to grow spiritually *(2 Timothy 2:15)*. You should avoid reading books that will seek to go against the word of God. There are so many false doctrines or teaching. To live victoriously as a Christian, you should ask God for wisdom and avoid "erroneous" teachings that may lead you away from your Christian faith.

6) PRAY TO GOD. Think of Him as your best friend. He loves you. You can tell Him anything and everything. *(1 Thessalonians 5:11, Mark 1:35)* You have to spend time with Him and make Him an active part of your daily life.

Prayer is vital to your spiritual growth. God is your heavenly Father and He wants to hear from you and have daily fellowship with you. Not only does He promise to answer your prayers, but as you pray, He will provide guidance and spiritual strength. The Bible tells us to "Pray continually," that is to pray faithfully every day *(1 Thessalonians 5:17).*

Here's how to be heard....

a) Pray with faith, using the Word of God *(Hebrews 11:6)*.

b) Always pray with clean hands and a pure heart *(Psalm 24:3)* Pray heartfelt, passionate prayers rather than vain repetitions *(Matthew 6:7)*.

c) Make sure that you are praying to the God revealed in the Holy Scriptures *(Exodus 20:3)*. As far as God is concerned, if you belong to Jesus, you are a representative of His Heavenly Kingdom. You can boldly come before the throne of Grace *(Hebrews 4:16)*. You have access to the King because you are the son or daughter of the King.

7) ADD TIMES OF FASTING TO YOUR PRAYER. As you pray, also spend time fasting. Fasting helps you to discipline your flesh. Naturally, your flesh does not want to obey God, but always remember dieting is not fasting. True fasting is spent acknowledging God while abstaining from certain foods & activities. Fasting along with praying and reading your Bible, helps you to keep your flesh and the attitudes of the flesh subjected to the Spirit of God. As a result, you will follow the leading of the Spirit of God more than you will obey your carnal, unrejuvenated desires.

8) PRAISE & WORSHIP. Praise and Worship are an important part of the believer's lifestyle. Your ability to praise God attracts His presence to your life. Your ability to worship keeps Him there. God loves a true worshipper. In **John 4:24**, the Word of God reveals that they who worship the Father must worship Him in spirit and in truth; for these are the people that God seeks out. The daily practice of praise and worship keeps Heaven open over your life and you position yourself to receive blessings, favor and increase from the Father because your worship pleases Him.

9) TAKE TIME TO FELLOWSHIP WITH OTHER CHRISTIANS. You are now in the Kingdom of God and you must regularly attend your church services and fellowship with God's people. *(Hebrews 10:15)*. Make sure the place you have called your church home calls sin what it is – **sin**. Do they believe the promises of God? Are they loving?   Does the pastor treat his wife with respect?   Is he a man of the Word? Does he have a humble heart and a gentle spirit? Listen closely to His teaching. **It should glorify God, magnify Jesus, and edify the believer.**   You will know you have been truly saved when you have a love for other Christians *(1 John 3:14).* As a result, you will want to fellowship with them.   The old saying, "Birds of a feather flock together" is true of Christians.

- You gather together for a time of fellowship and the breaking of bread or the ordinance of communion; for teaching from the Word of God; for praising and worshipping our God and for fellowship.

- You should attend your local church services regularly so that your faith can be strengthened by the preaching and teaching of God's Word.

- Further, you can also grow spiritually and be encouraged by the fellowship of other Christians.

- Church is where you go to express your love, faithfulness and worship to God. The Bible says, *"Not forsaking the assembling of ourselves together, as the manner of some is;" (Hebrews 10:25)*

10) WITNESS TO OTHERS. You must be willing to tell others about the great things that God has done and is doing in your life. This is called "WITNESSING" *(Matthew 28:19-20)*. It is important for you to openly declare Jesus Christ as your Savior and Lord to others, as it establishes the testimony of your faith. Once you have accepted Jesus Christ, tell someone. Do not keep it a secret. The Bible says, *"Whoever acknowledges me before men, I will also acknowledge him before my Father in heaven; But whoever (denies) disowns me before men, I will disown before my Father in heaven" (Matthew 10:32-33).*

11) LEARN HOW TO GIVE YOUR TITHE AND SOW SEEDS OR LOVE GIFTS. The Bible encourages us to give a tithe and an offering. This comes with a promise (read *Malachi 3:8-10).* It was once said that the wallet is the "last frontier." It is the final area to be conquered -- the last thing that comes to God in surrender. Jesus spoke much about money. He said that we cannot serve God and mammon *(Matthew 6:24).* The word "mammon" was the common Aramaic word for riches. In other words, we cannot trust God and money. Either money is our source of life, our great love, our joy, our sense of security, the supplier of our needs -- or God is.

When you open your purse or wallet, give generously and regularly to your local church. A guide as to how much you should give can be found in the "tithe" of the Old Testament, which is 10% of your income or increase. When you give your tithe, make sure you also give something to the work of God (see *Malachi 3:8-10), as an offering.* Give because you want to not because you have to. *God loves cheerful givers (2 Corinthians 9:7),* so learn to hold your money with a loose hand.

12) OBEDIENCE IS PARAMOUNT.

It is important to do what God's word is telling you because it will lead you to the right path and save you from destruction **(James 1:22-27)**. Lest we get the wrong idea, we are not the sovereign masters of our fate.

Only God is sovereign. He has chosen to give us a free will, and in giving us this free will, we are able to choose between good and evil. When we make the right choice according to God's Word, we are being obedient, and in our obedience, we are blessed.

"Obey your father and mother, that your days may be long in the land" (Exodus 20:12). The Lord God will give you long life if you are obedient to your earthly parents, so much more will He give you when you are obedient to Him.

13) ENGAGE IN WATER BAPTISM BY SUBMERSION. The Bible states, *"Repent and be baptized, every one of you, in the name of Jesus Christ for the remission of sins..." (Acts*

2:38). Water Baptism is a public declaration of your new life in Christ having buried the *old* you and witness of the *new you* who by faith is now alive in Christ Jesus *(Colossians 2:12).* There is therefore, no question as to whether or not you should be baptized. The questions are how, when, and by whom?

It would also seem clear from scripture that those who were baptized were fully immersed in water. Reason being, if John the Baptist was merely sprinkling believers, he would have had no need to baptize people in a river. In **Acts 16:25-40**, the Philippian jailer and his family were baptized at midnight as soon as they believed. Therefore, as you are now a believer, you are qualified for water baptism. Speak to your Pastor or spiritual leader in order to set a time for you to be baptized.

14) FIGHT THE GOOD FIGHT OF FAITH.

Now that you are growing and developing as a believer, you must learn how to maintain your walk with God. Many times the enemy will try to cause you to give up, to lose hope and to even go back to your former way of life. But you must continually resist the devil and use your spiritual weapons to "fight for your faith." In **1 Timothy 6:12**, we are encouraged to, *"Fight the good fight of faith, lay hold on eternal life, whereunto thou art also called, ..." There is an eternal reward for all those who endure to the end.*

Do not allow any temporary circumstance distract you from your eternal goal which is living in the presence of God for all eternity.

CHAPTER SIX

◀◆▶

THE FIGHT FOR YOUR SOUL

As a Christian, you must always remember that you are engaged in a relentless war that is taking place in the realm of the spirit. This war is being fought between the kingdom of darkness led by the devil and the kingdom of light led by Jehovah God and is for the ultimate possession of your soul.

Each kingdom functions similarly to earthly kingdoms as:

- It operates under established laws

- It seeks to protect and fortify itself

- It advances its interests while gaining new territories.

These spiritual kingdoms have already been established in the realm of the spirit. They now seek to become established in the earth realm. Every human being must choose whether they will serve the kingdom of light or the kingdom of darkness; good or evil; God or the devil. There is no neutral ground. When Jesus taught His disciples to pray, in *Matthew 6:10*, He taught them how to ask the Father for His kingdom to be established in earth even as it is in heaven.

"Thy kingdom come, thy will be done on earth as it is in heaven."

Also, in the book of *Revelation 11:15,* it states:

"The kingdoms of this world shall become the kingdoms of our Lord and of His Christ and He shall reign forever and ever."

Paul encourages the believers by saying *"Finally, my brethren, be strong in the Lord, and in the power of his might."* He went on to say, *"Put on the whole armor of God that you may be able to stand against the wiles of the devil." Ephesians 6:10, 11*

> *To stand* is a military word which means to stay your position; not to crumble, falter, fail or fall in your moment of test.

> *Against* is another military word, which signifies that you are not

with the enemy, but are in direct combat or opposition to them.

The "wiles of the devil" represents the plots, plans, and strategies that Satan has set up in an attempt to destroy you. The wiles further represent the arrows and missiles that he has set in place to be hurled against your anointing.

THE WHOLE ARMOR

Since we are living in the last days, it is incumbent upon each believer to put on the whole armor of God. Having on the whole armor protects you from the wiles of the devil and equips you for spiritual warfare. You cannot go to fight unless you are appropriately attired. God gives us a spiritual dress code that we must all wear daily.

"Put on the whole armour of God so that you can stand against the wiles of the devil." (Ephesians 6:11)

The whole armor includes the following:

1. *The Helmet of Salvation* – you must be born again. The helmet protects your head which is your mind. Satan will try to attack your mind to destroy you.

2. *The Breastplate of Righteousness* – this speaks to your holy character and moral conduct. The breastplate protects the most critical area, which is your heart.

"It is with the heart one believes unto righteousness." (Romans 10:10)

"The righteous are as bold as a lion." (Proverbs 28:1)

"Keep (guard) your heart with all diligence, for out of it are the issues of life." (Proverbs. 4:23)

3. *The Shield of Faith* – this depicts your utmost confidence and trust in God. This shield was used to protect the entire body, soul and spirit from Satan's devices and extinguishes the fiery darts of the enemy.

4. *The Sword of the Spirit* – the Word of God. *"study to show yourself approved unto God."* Rhema, in the Greek, means the spoken Word. The Word of God is one of the most

powerful weapons against the enemy.

5. *The Girdle of Truth* – helps us to live with integrity and honesty.

6. *Feet shod with Preparation of the Gospel of Peace " –thy word is a lamp unto my feet and a light unto my path." (Psalm 119:105)* Shoes represent your ability or your destiny. Therefore, you must take the Word of God everywhere you go in a spirit of peace and love.

7. *All Prayer and Supplication – the effectual fervent prayer of the righteous man availeth much (James 5:16b).*

Prayer is another very powerful weapon against the enemy and is very effective, if employed properly.

It is not God's will that you spend every second of the day fighting demons. However, because you may constantly encounter the enemy, you should be equipped to disarm and destroy his arsenals.

CHAPTER SEVEN

———◄|♦|►———

DELIVERANCE IS THE
CHILDREN'S BREAD

As you begin your new life in Christ, you will soon learn that God has many benefits for His children. One such benefit God has reserved for the people who believe in Him is deliverance.

In order for you to walk in your deliverance, you must be willing to *acknowledge* that there is an issue in your life. Identify, assess and diagnose your true issues. You must then decide that you are now ready to be set totally free from the demonic strongholds tormenting

your life and let them go. In order
to gain your deliverance, you must
be willing to practice the following:

- Pray in the name of Jesus, standing
in the authority of His blood.

- Repent of any sin that has resulted
in a curse being placed over your
life – sins you may have committed
or even sins that your ancestors
may have committed (which may
include covenants, pacts, vows,
agreements, and the like)

- Summon holy angelic assistance
according to **Psalm 103:20-22** to
stand guard and warfare on your
behalf

- Break all curses, pacts, agreements,
etc., including generational or
ancestral curses back to the

fifteenth generation or as far back as you may feel is necessary

• Denounce and break soul ties, witchcraft spells, or any other contrary or negative practices

• It is important that you understand that *"even though we walk in the flesh, we do not war after the flesh."* For the weapons of our warfare are not carnal but are mighty through God to the pulling down of strongholds (2 Corinthians 10:3,4).*

" Behold I have given unto you power (authority) over all the powers (abilities, tactics or plans) of the enemy.
(Luke 10:19)

God has truly given you power over all of the evil powers of the enemy. There should be nothing that the enemy sends your way that you are not able to overcome. In order to remain victorious during times when the enemy is coming up against your life, you must:

1.*Identify and expose what is attacking you;* You must identify what strategy the enemy is using to come against your life. Remember, his goal is to steal, kill and destroy your life, especially your walk with God. (John 10:10) He does not want you to enjoy your life as a Christian and he does not want you fulfilling the will of God for your life.

2.*Pray with Power* – You must rebuke or stop the attack of the enemy through prayer. The

Word of God teaches in James 5:16, that the effectual, fervent prayer of the righteous availeth much. Prayer is one of the most powerful weapons given to the Believer. Once you learn how to pray effectively, you will be able to defeat every attack of the enemy; right on your knees.

3.***Speak the Word of God*** *– in addition to prayer, you can also release the Word of God and scriptures in the atmosphere. During challenging times, it is very important that you know the Word and you declare it with boldness and accuracy (Proverbs 18:21). I would encourage you to play the audio Bible throughout your room on* a continual basis. Get as much of the word as you can; knowing the Word will give you what to say to defeat every attack of the enemy. During Jesus' time of being tempted by the devil, He declared the written Word against every temptation the enemy sent against Him. (Matthew 4:1 - 11)

4. **Hold on to Every prophetic Word God has given you** – During seasons of testing and trial you must recall every prophecy that God has ever spoken to you. This will give you confidence and assurance that God loves you and has powerful plans for your life.

5.*Call on angelic assistance –*
*The more you grow in faith you
will begin to understand the
Ministry of God's holy angels.
God gave us the power to
command His holy angels. You
can call for angelic assistance
because the Word of God says
that there are angels which
excel in strength, hearkening to
the voice of your commands.
You can dispatch angels to
warfare on your behalf.*
(Psalm 103:20)

6.**Apply the blood of Jesus –**
*Jesus came and shed every drop
of His blood on Calvary so that
you may, not only be saved, but
that you can live an abundant
life, free from every yoke of*

bondage of the enemy. You must appropriate, apply and plead the blood of Jesus specifically to your situation; when you do, this will remind the enemy that he is already defeated in your life and the blood of Jesus frees you from his yoke of bondage.

How do you plead or apply the blood to your life? You pray this audibly: "Father God I plead/ apply the Blood of Jesus Christ over my life." Even though you are now saved, you are simply asking God to keep you covered and protected by the Blood of Jesus.

7. **Release and declare the Name of Jesus** *You have to call on the*

name of Jesus because He has all power, even over death. Just the mention of His name releases that same power in the atmosphere and every demonic spirit of death will have to go **(Matthew 28:18).**

8. **Endure until the end** – *You must predetermine you are going to endure until the end of your test and that you are going to come out victorious. Although, you do not know when God is going to deliver you, you must remain resolute that He can and He will. The Word of God declares in in* **Matthew 24:13; "But he that shall endure unto the end, the same shall be**

saved"; the glory is in the finish.

9.**Release the power of God to operate** *in your life by declaring and activating the Word of God.*

Many people make the mistake in believing that the only reason the enemy is fighting them is because they are a Christian. Although, he seeks to target Christians more so than unbelievers, he still attacks their lives as well. The difference between you, a Christian, and the non-believer is that you have powerful spiritual weapons given to you by God to defeat every attack of the adversary against your life. God the Father loved you so much, He sent His Son to die for you. Jesus Christ, Son of the Living God, loved you so much, that He took on human flesh, sacrificed His life by shedding every drop of blood in His body so that you can live.

Jesus gave us the Holy Spirit who would teach us all things and lead us in the pathway that would take us through righteous paths while here on earth and all the way to Heaven. Accepting Jesus Christ as your Lord and Savior was the best decision you could ever make. Now and for all eternity!

Jesus died so that you could have eternal life. Salvation is a free gift from God...accepting Him today will help you begin living your best life now and forever!

PROPHETESS DR. MATTIE
NOTTAGE BA, MA, DD
MINISTRY   PROFILE

---◄┤♦├►---

Widely endorsed as a prophet to the nations, God has used Dr. Mattie Nottage to captivate audiences around the world through her insightful, life-changing messages.

Dr. Nottage is married to Apostle Edison Nottage. She co-pastors, along with her husband, Believers Faith Outreach Ministries, International in Nassau, Bahamas.

Mantled by the Spirit of God with an undeniable gift of discernment and an undeniable prophetic anointing, Dr. Nottage is a highly sought after, well-respected international preacher, prolific teacher, motivational speaker, life coach, playwright, author, gospel recording artist and revivalist. She is the President and Founder of *Mattie Nottage Ministries, International,*

The Global Dominion Network Empowering Group of Companies, The Youth In Action Group and The Faith Village For Girls Transformation Program. She is also The Chancellor of The Mattie Nottage School of Ministry. She is the Founder of the prestigious Mattie Nottage Outstanding Kingdom Woman's Award.

Dr. Nottage has ministered the gospel, in places such as: Ireland, Brazil, Africa, The Netherlands, throughout the United States of America and The Caribbean. Gifted with an authentic anointing, God uses her to "set the captive free" and to fan the flames of revival throughout the nations. Dr. Mattie Nottage, has an endearing passion to train and equip individuals to advance the Kingdom of God and walk in total victory. She is the author of her bestselling books, ***"Breaking The Chains, From Worship to Warfare"***, ***"I Refuse To Die"*** and ***"Secrets Every Mother Should Tell Her Daughter About Life"*** Book & Journal.

Dr. Nottage is also a regular

columnist in The Tribune, the national newspaper of the Bahamas. She has also written numerous publications, stage plays and songs, including the #1 smash hit CD Singles, *"I Refuse To Die In This Place!"*, *"The Verdict Is In...Not Guilty!"* and *"I Still Want You!"* She has regularly appeared as a guest on various television networks including The Trinity Broadcasting Network (TBN), The Word Network, The Atlanta Live TV and The Babbie Mason Talk Show "Babbie's House" amongst others. Additionally, Dr. Mattie Nottage has been featured in several magazine publications such as the Preaching Woman Magazine and the "Gospel Today" Magazine as one of America's most influential pastors. She, along with her husband, Apostle Edison are the hosts of their very own television show, "Transforming Lives" which airs weekly on The Impact Network.

Dr. Nottage is the former Chairman of the National Youth Advisory Council to the government of the Bahamas and was also recognized and awarded a

"Proclamation of State" by the Mayor and Commissioner of Miami-Dade County, Florida for her exemplary community initiatives that bring transformation and empowerment to the lives of youth and families globally. Further, Dr. Nottage has earned her, Bachelor of Arts degree in Christian Counseling, a Masters of Arts degree in Christian Education, and a Doctor of Divinity degree from the renown St. Thomas University, in Jacksonville, Florida and is also a graduate of Kingdom University. Additionally, she has earned her Certified Life-Coaching Degree from the F. W. I. Life Coach Training Institute. Dr. Mattie Nottage is known as a Trailblazer and a *"Doctor of Deliverance"* who is committed and dedicated to *Breaking Chains and Transforming Lives*!

PROPHETESS DR.
MATTIE NOTTAGE
BOOKS & CD'S
For Spiritual Growth
BEST SELLING BOOK
NEWLY RELEASED BOOK AND AUDIO CD
BREAKING THE CHAINS
I REFUSE TO DIE
I STILL WANT YOU
THE CALL TO A DEEPER PLACE
PRAYER FOR THE ANNIHILATION AND ASSASINATION OF MY ENEMIES
BOOK & AUDIO PRAYER
12 MINUTES TO BREAKTHROUGH PRAYER STRATEGY
NEWLY RELEASED SINGLE HIT CD'S
MENDING THE MARRIAGE
SECRETS EVERY MOTHER SHOULD TELL HER DAUGHTER ABOUT LIFE
SECRETS EVERY MOTHER SHOULD TELL HER DAUGHTER ABOUT LIFE
DESTINY
MUSIC CD/MUSIC VIDEO
LIKE FIRE
MUSIC CD/MUSIC VIDEO
WORSHIP EXPERIENCE
A SHIFT IN SEASON
MUSIC CD
I REFUSE TO DIE
I STILL WANT YOU
MUSIC CD/MUSIC VIDEO
REVIVAL IS HERE
MUSIC CD
www.mattienottage.org | www.amazon.com | iTUNES.com
ON SALE NOW! >> 888.825.7568 | 242.812.1070 | 242.698.1383
YouTube
CONNECT & SUBSCRIBE TO:
MATTIENOTTAGE TV
TRANSFORMING LIVES TV
USA - 6511 Nova Dr. Ste 193, Davie Florida 33317-7401
BAH - P.O. Box SB-52524 Nassau, Bahamas